CONTENTS

Printed in the United States of America
First Printing, 2011
ISBN-13: 978-1463680633
Maine College Press, Inc.
P.O. Box 351
Orono, ME 04473

tackling-football.com

SECTION I:

INTRODUCTION

Why we did the book:

As we celebrate nearly 40 years since the passage of **Title IX**, we recognize that women's participation and interest in sports has increased. Women are not only fans, but also players, cheerleaders, trainers, reporters, sports information directors, and coaches, and on occasion, officials, commentators, and athletic directors. There is no question that women have become more knowledgeable and involved in sports.

Looking specifically at football, one of America's most popular sports, we see many women among the millions of people who crowd stadiums or watch games on television. Yet our experience shows that most women football fans (and some men football fans, for that matter) are not well-versed enough in the intricacies of football. Most are avid spectators, but not *knowledgeable*, avid football spectators. Certainly there are some women who understand all the ins and outs of the game. For example, with the popularity of college football and its exposure on television — including the play-by-play, color commentary, analysis and in-depth interviews — it would be almost impossible not to learn something from the broadcast. Yet many more women do not have a basic understanding of the game. This is not due to a lack of interest. In fact, many college women are enthusiastic about the game and want to learn more, but there are few resources available.

Tackling Football: A Woman's Guide to Understanding the College Game provides women with the basics for understanding a college football game — how it is played, including the various playing positions, and basic offensive and defensive strategies. It includes a close-up look at what happens before, during, and after the game, as well as how to listen to a play-by-play. It is written in a "user-friendly" format and is drawn from our combined years of experience with college football as spectator, player and coach.

We feel that *few things in sports compare to the excitement of a weekend college football game* — from socializing with friends at the pregame tailgating parties to the energy of the crowd cheering their team's touchdown over a rival. We want others to have that experience and share in our love and appreciation for the game.

Basic explanation of the game

Football is an easy game overall involving strength, skill, and strategy. It consists of two teams of 11 players. The team that has possession of the ball (the **offense**) tries to move the ball to the other team's end zone to score points, either by a touchdown or a field goal. They have 4 chances (or **downs**) to move the ball 10 yards using a pre-designed strategy called a **play**. If they are successful in gaining 10 yards (or more), it is called a **first down**, and they get another 4 chances to move the ball another 10 yards. Meanwhile, the other team tries to stop them (which is why they are called the **defense**). The team that scores the most points wins. One thing you'll notice is that the game stops after every play. This allows the teams to call a new play. While the rules and strategies for how each team will move the ball (the offense) or stop the ball (the defense) are the most complicated of any sport, if you understand the basics, you can follow along and enjoy the game.

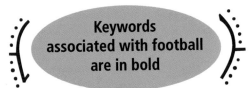

Keywords associated with football are in bold

SECTION 11:

BEFORE THE SEASON BEGINS

College football differs from professional football

This book focuses on the college game. By understanding the college football game, one can certainly follow a professional game because the rules of how to play are very similar. However, what differs between college and professional football concerns things much bigger than what happens on the field on game day. While professional football involves a few dozen teams (franchises) based in major cities, and is associated with Monday night games, the draft, professional athletes with contracts and agents, the Super Bowl, and the Hall of Fame, *college football* involves hundreds of teams playing at all different skill levels on college campuses across the country, and is associated with such things as school fight songs, traditions, Saturday afternoon games, student-athletes, post-season Bowl games, All-American teams and the Heisman Trophy.

While professional football is big business and governed by the **National Football League**, college football is governed by the **National Collegiate Athletic Association (NCAA)** and they determine much of what happens before the season even begins.

The NCAA sets the rules for college football

The **NCAA** is the governing body for most college sports. Within this organization, the **NCAA Football Rules Committee** determines the rules for playing football. The rules for football have changed dramatically since the first known college game was played between Princeton and Rutgers in New Brunswick, N.J. in 1869. At that time, the game resembled something more like rugby. As the game has evolved, so have the rules. A good example is the bat-ball play, last used in 1978 by the University of Maine to tie a game against the University of New Hampshire. It involved the kicker batting the ball (instead of kicking it for a field goal) into the end zone where a teammate pounced on it to score. This was a legitimate play under a little-known rule that allowed batting a backward pass for the purpose of gaining yardage as long as the ball stayed inbounds. The NCAA later removed this play from the rules.

The NCAA also determines when you can start **pre-season practice**, which is based on your first game of the season. For example, the NCAA specifies each team is allowed 27 practice sessions before their opening game. Teams are also allowed 15 **spring practice** sessions. The **regular season** typically begins at the end of August and runs through early December. A team plays one game against conference opponents, plus a few other games against teams outside their conference. The team with the best record in their conference at the end of the season is the champion.

Beyond stipulating the rules of the college game and practice, the NCAA also has rules governing such things as **eligibility** (including **red-shirting**), financial aid and expenditures, athletic certification, academic progress toward a degree, and recruitment of student-athletes. The NCAA publishes a detailed manual of administrative rules to guide coaches and

institutions on the "who, what, where, and when" for running their college athletic program.

Schools are divided into three divisions and the NCAA limits the number of athletic scholarships awarded to schools in each division.

1. The top schools are **Division I** and give out the most scholarships. This division is divided into two groups: Football Bowl Subdivision for teams selected to play in bowl games after the regular season, and Football Championship Subdivision in which teams can qualify for a post-season tournament. Besides players on scholarships, there may also be students who made the team but have not been awarded athletic scholarships (referred to as **walk-ons**). In many cases, Division I football programs generate enough revenue to support most of the other sports within their athletic department.

Division II offers approximately half the number of athletic scholarships, and **2.**

3. **Division III** schools have the smaller football programs and do not offer athletic scholarships.

Within each division, colleges are further divided into regional conferences. There are also some schools that do not belong to any conference (they are known as **Independents**). Every week, polls determine ranking of teams within their division based on wins-losses and the difficulty of their opponents. This helps determine post-season play.

Preparing for the big game

When you arrive on Saturday to watch the game, it is important to appreciate how much time and energy the coaches and players have devoted to mentally and physically preparing for this one contest. As you watch the game, it becomes apparent that strength and conditioning plays a vital role in the success of the player and, ultimately, the team.

Each team has a playbook,

with a variety of plays that have been practiced throughout the week before the big game. These are strategies for moving the ball down the field or stopping the other team from moving the ball. Football players are recruited to play college football because of their athletic ability (e.g., kick, pass, run, catch), so the majority of practice time is devoted to the details of executing various plays. Coaches work seven days a week — from Sunday morning to Kickoff on Saturday — to get their players ready for the game. A critical component involves watching and analyzing video of the other team in action to prepare for playing against their opponent in the game.

SECTiON lll:

BEFORE THE GAME

Be sure to arrive at the game early to check out the place, the people, and, of course, the **tailgating**. In a designated area of the stadium parking lot, you will see groups of people gathered around car tailgates. This is the "pre-party" where people socialize with friends over food and drink before the game. Make sure you have your ticket; it will be marked for either **reserve seating** (the better seats) or **general admission**.

The place — as you go through the gate, take a look around. Pay particular attention to the field, scoreboard, and stadium.

The Field

All football fields are positioned north to south so that the sun is less likely to be in the players' direct line of vision. Traditional fields are made of **natural grass**. Modern fields have synthetic turf filled with a mixture of tiny rubber pellets and sand, which creates a grass-like playing surface. Such an **artificial turf** surface eliminates poor playing conditions on rain-soaked sod.

The field is rectangular - 100 yards long and 52 yards wide. The **sidelines** and **end lines** are the boundaries of the field. Step on or over these lines and you are out of bounds. The **50-yard line** splits the field. Numbers are printed on the field every 10 yards. These numbers decrease from 50 as they approach each **goal line** at either end. Two sets of **hash marks** run end-to-end indicating each yard line. When the ball is ready for play, it is placed on or inside these hash marks at the spot where the previous play ended.

The **end zone**, located at either end of the field, is 10 yards deep, bordered by the **goal line** and end line. To score a touchdown, the ball must cross the goal line. Bright orange **pylons** are placed at the corners of the end zone and along the end line to help define the end zone.

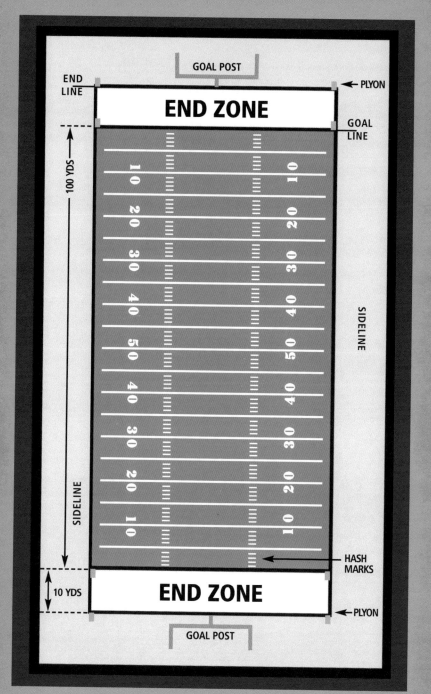

Goal posts are placed on each end line. A team scores by kicking the ball through these goal posts, running the ball into the end zone or catching a pass in the end zone.

On the sideline opposite the press box, you will see two bright orange metal poles with a 10-yard chain attached. The **chain** marks the distance needed to achieve the 10 yards (a first down). There is also a **down marker,** which indicates where the player with the ball was tackled, stopping the play, and which down is being played: first, second, third or fourth down. If you feel lost or are unsure what is happening during the game, look for the people operating the chains (called the **chain gang**).

Also on the sideline is the **ball** used to play the game. A football historically was made of pig leather and explains why it is still referred to as a "**pigskin**." The football is shaped to make it more efficient for throwing **forward passes**. It is brown, made of leather, and has white lace on one side to help with grip.

The Scoreboard

The **scoreboard** tells you a lot about what's going on in the game — who has possession of the ball, where the ball is, what down it is, how much time is left in the period, and, most important, the score. The football icon next to the score (**HOME** or **GUEST**) indicates which team has the ball. The small number next to the score indicates how many **time outs left (TOL)** the team has remaining to use (they have 3 time outs each half). **Period** signals which quarter is being played: 1 through 4. **Ball on** tells you what yard line the ball is presently on. **Down** indicates which of the four downs is presently being played (first through fourth); **YDS To Go** indicates the number of yards needed for another first down.

Football is played in four 15-minute quarters (two quarters per half)

The clock counts down how much time is left in the quarter. The teams switch sides at the end of the first and third quarters. At the half, teams are off the field for 20 minutes.

The Scoreboard

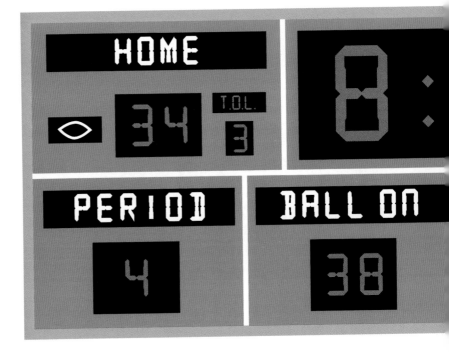

The average college football game lasts about 3 hours because the **clock stops** for a variety of reasons including: the ball carrier goes out of bounds, there is a penalty, a player is injured, a pass is incomplete, someone scores, a time-out is called, or the quarter ends. Otherwise, the clock keeps running.

There is also a **40-second play clock** that starts counting down the time from the end of the previous play to the next, ensuring that the game is moving along and not being delayed (which would lead to a **delay of game penalty** against the offense).

Stadium

The home team sideline

is on the press box side of the field. Playing at your home stadium creates what is known as the **home field advantage.** Players are familiar with their surroundings and the stadium is filled with friendly fans who control the noise during the game. Plus, visiting players are sometimes tired from travel and change of routine.

The **press box** serves four main purposes: It provides a reporting venue for the media, as well as scoreboard operators and official statisticians; it has separate rooms for coaches to observe and direct the game from a superior vantage point above the field; it offers a weatherproof area for video and TV cameras to record the game — video players and coaches use later for instruction and analysis; and there are also private venues or **skyboxes** for VIP's, such as the university President, major donors, alumni, sponsors, or other dignitaries.

As you look around the stadium, you can't help but notice all the signs around the field advertising local, regional, and national businesses. These are **corporate sponsors** who have paid money to the athletic department for this ad space. With tight budgets and rising

GO TEAM!

expenditures, most college sports programs could not operate without the revenue from these outside financial resources. One can understand the concern that for some colleges, sports have become more like a business.

The People

As you head to your seat, you'll notice that many of the fans are wearing their team's colors. When considering what you'll wear to the game, do not make the mistake of wearing the colors of the opposing team.

Dress comfortably, and bring warmer clothes

(including a hat and gloves) as it may get colder as the sun goes down. Some fans will even go so far as to paint the school's colors on their face, while others may be holding signs or waving pom-poms. Take a moment to look around at the people on or near the field. Pay special attention to the officials, coaches, and players, as well as other important people on the sidelines.

Officials

Seven officials are assigned to every game. They watch the interaction between players on the field and make sure the rules are followed. They maintain order. They are easy to spot because they wear uniforms: black and white striped shirts, white pants, and baseball caps. Each has specific duties and stands in a particular area of the field to watch certain groups of players. For example:

1. The **referee** is the head official; he wears the white hat and announces the penalties.

2. The **umpire** lines up behind the line of scrimmage to monitor the play; the umpire also keeps track of time outs, the coin toss, and the score.

3. The **head linesman** straddles the line of scrimmage from the sidelines to monitor plays; he works closely with the chain gang to measure distance.

4. The **line judge** stands across the field from the head linesman and monitors the quarterback and the timing of the game.

5. The **back judge** stands in the defensive backfield to monitor play; he is the official on field goals, standing under the goalpost to rule whether a kick is good.

6. & 7. Others in the backfield include the **field judge** and **side judge** who also monitor the play.

Each official has a whistle to blow to let everyone know the ball is dead,

meaning play has stopped. Each official also has a **yellow flag** that he drops where a foul has occurred, which is why it is also known as a **penalty marker**. Once a flag is dropped, the officials gather on the field to sort out what happened and determine the penalty. The referee announces the foul, along with the number of the player who committed the foul; he also uses hand signals to indicate the foul committed.

The coaching staff is typically made up of 11 coaches.

The **head coach** is responsible for every aspect of the football program year-round, on and off the field. Next to the university's President, he is often the most recognized figure at that university. In Division I, he may be the highest paid employee. An **Offensive Coordinator**, who usually coaches the quarterbacks, assists him on offense. There are also assistant coaches who work directly with each position in the offense — running backs, wide receivers, offensive line, and tight ends. On defense there is also a **Defensive Coordinator** who usually coaches the linebackers. There are also position coaches for the defensive line, as well as the safeties and cornerbacks, collectively known as defensive backs. One coach on the staff is usually assigned to be responsible for all special teams play. There are also usually two graduate assistant coaches, one on offense and one on defense, who are attending graduate school while they are coaching.

Schools in the smaller divisions have fewer coaches. For example, in Division III there are usually only six coaches on each staff. This means the head coach must assume a coaching responsibility along with all his other responsibilities. The other coaches may coach two positions, and special team responsibilities are usually distributed among several coaches.

• •

The head coach not only organizes his coaches and practice schedules for the season, but also is responsible for alumni relations and development, the academic progress of his students, community relations and service, and recruiting high school student-athletes for future seasons.

• •

During the season, no matter what Division, coaches usually work an 80-hour workweek. In preparing for each game, they must watch and analyze each opponent's video play-by-play. With input from the other assistants, the coordinators are responsible for organizing and creating the final **game plan** of plays. Within the head coach's master schedule, they also create every aspect of practice for the week. Each position coach will then create a detailed plan within the individual segments of practice. The players will generally meet with their **position coach** each day in a classroom setting for about an hour and a half before practice to review the plan and watch video of the opponent.

On game day, each coach is responsible for the performance of his position players.

Each coordinator will direct the offensive or defensive plan as laid out and practiced during the week. These coordinators usually coach from the press box so they have a better overall view of the game. They communicate with the assistant coaches on the sideline via **headphones.** This way, they can communicate any adjustments that may need to be made during the game based on what the coaches in the press box are seeing.

The offense and defense use two different sets of headphones so communication is clear and not interfering with the other. The head coach usually has headphones that can switch back and forth between the two so he can keep track of the flow of the game and make any changes he thinks necessary.

At halftime, teams have 20 minutes to rest in the locker room. At this time, the coaches will meet to discuss any second half adjustments that need to be made on offense and defense. Then position coaches will communicate these adjustments to their players.

Half Time

This 20-minute break between halves allows the players time to recover and the coaches a chance to adjust strategies. It also gives the fans a chance to:
- return to tailgating to socialize and talk about how the game is going.
- visit the concessions. Stadium food (e.g., hotdogs, nachos, popcorn) is a part of the game-day experience.
- watch the halftime show, which typically involves the marching band, cheerleaders, majorettes, and dancers.

Coaching is a year-round job and recruiting the best players is critical for the success of the program. Each coach is assigned a particular **recruiting territory** and is responsible to know about every **prospect** in his area.

The NCAA regulates every aspect of recruiting — from phone calls, to coaches' travel to see prospects, and prospect opportunities to visit colleges.

Coaches spend countless hours, 365 days a year, working to find the best recruits and convince them to attend their university. Recruiting is the life blood of every football program because great players mean more wins and this makes their coaches look great. Knowing that coaching offers no real job security (they can be let go at any time), wins can help ensure that coaches get to keep their job for next season.

Players

I f you arrive early enough before the game, you will see the players warming up. They all exit the field after the warm-up drills for the final pep talk by the head coach. They return before the start of the game to cheers from the crowd as the game is about to get under way. The players have different roles and positions. This helps you understand when they will be on the field and where they will stand once they get out there.

The offense is made up of 11 men who are on the field when they have possession of the ball and are trying to score points.

The defense is made up of 11 players who are on the field when the other team has the ball; their job is to stop the other team from moving the ball down the field and scoring points. These two groups of players are on the field the most. Their specific positions will be described later.

There are also special teams who play when the ball is kicked during the game.

These special teams include:

- The **kickoff team** and **kickoff return team** who come onto the field at the start of the game and the start of the second half, and after every score. Their efforts determine where the play will begin.

- The **punt team** and **punt return team** who come onto the field when the offense has failed to achieve a first down and will decide to kick the ball to the other team.

Throughout the game, you will see lots of players running off and on the field, based on who has possession of the ball. Offensive team players wait on the sidelines while the players on the defensive team try to stop the opponent who has possession of the ball. Once they regain possession of the ball, all the offensive players run onto the field and all the defensive players run off the field.

Players are also identified by how often they play:

◎ **First team** refers to those who play the most.

◎ **Second team** are those who play only if someone is tired/injured.

◎ **Practice players** are those who practice but do not play in the game.

• •

Between the first and second team of offensive and defensive players, and the players on the various special teams, it is not unusual to see 100 football players on each team dressed and suited up for the game. All players wear a nylon team jersey with their number printed on the front and back. Some teams also put the player's last name on the back of the jersey. A dark jersey typically signifies the home team. Due to the very physical nature of the game, protective equipment is worn. Specifically, pads (shoulder, hip, thigh, tail, knee), and a **helmet with facemask** are required. New research linking concussions to brain injury has led to greater emphasis on the importance of the helmet and keeping players out of the game who have experienced a head injury. Other protection includes a mouth guard and athletic supporter. Players may also be seen wearing black shadow on their cheeks to protect them from the sun's glare.

Others on or around the sidelines

Besides the coaches, there are many players standing along the sidelines when it is not their turn to be on the field; they are called **reserve players**. Others may be **medical staff,** including team doctors and athletic trainers, **equipment staff** in case of equipment failure, the chain gang of three who hold and operate the chain and down marker, **electricians** in case the coaches' headphones go down, and media people, such as **photographers** and **videographers**.

Behind these people are those who add to the excitement and entertainment during the game: the **cheerleaders** who cheer on the team and help to get fans involved in chanting things like

"DEFENSE"!

when the other team has the ball, the **majorettes** twirling their batons, and the **marching band** that plays the national anthem, along with music to liven up the crowd (e.g, the school's fight song), and sometimes provides a drum roll with each kickoff.

Also wandering the sidelines and the stands are the team **mascot**, people selling food from the concessions, and those selling the **game day program**.

Besides being a great souvenir of the game, the program contains lots of useful information.

It lists the starting line up (those top 11 players on offense and defense), as well as the team roster of players with information on their position, number, age, height and weight, and hometown. It also contains a short synopsis of each team, statistics, the coaching staff, and corporate sponsorship information.

SECTION IV:

THE GAME

Following the playing of the national anthem and some general announcements, the game is ready to begin. But first you will see the **coin toss**, and then the **kickoff** before the game's real interaction takes place between the starting lineup of offensive versus defensive players. It's this interaction that typically leads to scoring, but also penalties.

Coin Toss

Team captains meet at the center of the field with the head official (in the white hat).

● ● ● ● ● ● ● ● ● ● ● ● ● ● ● ● ● ●

The visiting team calls heads or tails

● ● ● ● ● ● ● ● ● ● ● ● ● ● ● ● ● ●

to determine which team will make **the choice** at the beginning of the game or **defer** that choice until after the halftime break. The team that wins the toss can decide to make the choice after halftime (defer) or… make the choice now (receive or defend).

The team that is making the choice at the beginning of the first half has to decide whether to receive the kickoff and therefore possess the ball or to defend a particular end of the field. Or to put it another way: Do I want the ball? What side of the field do I want to play from (defend)?

If the team defers, the other team makes the choice to begin the game. If the winner of the coin toss decides to make the choice at that time, the other team makes their choice after halftime. This decision is frequently determined by wind conditions. Teams like to have the wind at their back to make it easier to pass or kick. If the wind is strong, the captain will choose to defer the choice to the second half so he can make sure that by choosing to defend a goal, the wind is at their back in the fourth quarter — an advantage in the event of a close game.

Kickoff

After the choice has been made, the team playing offense will receive a **kickoff** from the team designated to play defense.

This is the first play of the game.

The kickoff happens at the beginning of the first and second half of the game, and after every score. This is done by a special group of players who are on one of the special teams. The one group for the defense is trained in kickoff and the other special team on the field is the kickoff return team.

The ball is placed on a **kicking tee** (that holds the ball upright) at the 30-yard line. The kicker takes a running start to kick the ball as far as possible. Defenders line up across the field and cannot pass the 30-yard line until the ball is kicked. The team receiving the kick will assign the man closest to the **goal line** to catch and return the kick as far up field as possible. He needs to run as fast as he can to get as far as he can up the field. All other players will be assigned to block those on the kicking team who are trying to **tackle** the player running with the ball. **First Down and 10 Yards to Go** will begin where the kick returner who was running with the ball is stopped.

Let the game really begin. But who am I looking at and what are they supposed to be doing?

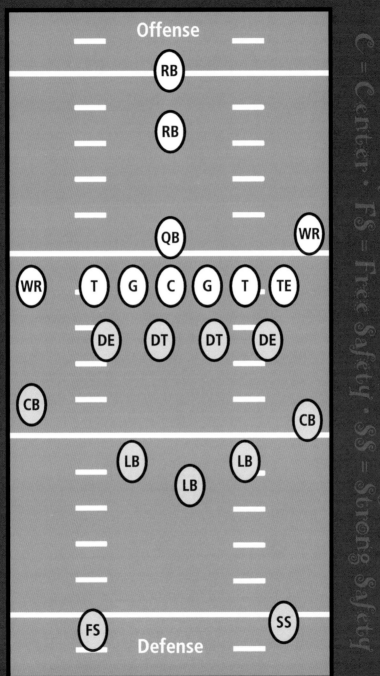

Offense

RB
RB
QB
WR
WR T G C G T TE
DE DT DT DE
CB
CB
LB LB
LB
FS SS

Defense

DE = Defensive End · DT = Defensive Tackle
CB = Corner Back · LB = Linebacker

T = Tackle · G = Guard · C = Center · FS = Free Safety · TE = Tight End · SS = Strong Safety

RB = Running Back · QB = Quarterback
WR = Wide Receiver

Players on Offense:

Move the ball toward the goal line and score!

Quarterback (QB): Leads and directs the offense, hands the ball to the RB's for runs, passes the ball to the WR's, TE's, and RB's.

Running Back (RB) - Runners: QB hands the ball to them to execute run plays. They also block for each other and will catch a pass from the QB at times.

Wide Receiver (WR), **Tight End** (TE) - Pass catcher: They will run down the field, past the line of scrimmage a set amount of yards to catch a pass from the QB then run toward the goal line. They also block on running plays. As a group, pass catchers are known as **Pass Receivers** or "Receivers" for short.

Offensive Line - Blockers: Push the defenders around to create openings between defensive players for the RB's to run through and protect the quarterback when throwing. There are five linemen who line up along the line of scrimmage. The **Center** (C) snaps the ball to the QB. There are two **Guards** (G) who line up on either side of the Center and the two **Tackles** (T) line up next to the Guards.

Players on Defense:

Stop the offense!
No first downs and no score!

Cornerback (CB), **Free Safety** (FS), **Strong Safety** (SS) - Pass stoppers: Don't let the pass catchers catch the ball. Tackle any runner who gets past the defenders at the line of scrimmage. Collectively, these players are known as **Defensive Backs**.

Linebacker (LB) - Don't let the runners run the ball. Cover any receiver close to the line of scrimmage. **Blitz** the QB on passing plays when directed by the coach. This means to attack and tackle the QB before he has the chance to throw the ball.

Defensive Tackle (DT)**, Defensive End** (DE) - Quarterback chasers: Don't let the quarterback throw the ball. Tackle any runner with the ball. This group of players is known as the **Defensive Line**.

Offense - We have the ball!

> **The offense is the team that has possession of the ball and attempts to score the points.**

These players are skilled in blocking, running with the ball, passing the ball, receiving the ball — skills that are practiced throughout the pre-season and in daily practice. Here are the basics to understand what they are doing and follow along:

First Down and 10 Yards to Go: To begin, the offense has four chances to get another first down and 10-yard opportunity.

Line of Scrimmage: This is where the ball is placed to begin each down. It is an imaginary line that stretches from sideline to sideline that runs through the ball. The line of scrimmage is the spot where the offensive player was tackled to the ground by the defense on the previous play.

The Snap: To begin a down, the ball is placed where the previous play finished. The next play will begin with the snap, which is the action of a lineman lifting the ball from the ground and handing it between his legs to the quarterback.

Out of Bounds: When a player with the ball crosses the sidelines, he is considered out of bounds and the play is stopped there. The result is as if he was tackled at that spot, creating a new line of scrimmage and a next down opportunity for the offense. Also, the game clock is stopped and will restart when the referee signals the ball is ready for play. However, in the final two minutes of each half, the clock will stop until the ball is snapped on the next play.

The Huddle: The offense or defense will gather together in the huddle to direct each player what to do and where to go. This is referred to as **calling the play**. It's also where the quarterback will tell the other players when the ball will be snapped during the **cadence**.

The Play: This is the specific alignment and action desired by the coaches during the upcoming down.

Starting Signal and Cadence: These are the words yelled by the quarterback to his players at the line of scrimmage. This communication is done in code and has several meanings. It tells his players what the defense is doing and, based on this, may change the play called in the huddle to a different play. It also signals when the snap will occur.

Offensive Formations, Alignments and Motion:

Each offensive formation must have at least 7 men aligned on the line of scrimmage. These are usually the 5 **offensive linemen**, the **tight end** and one of the **wide receivers**. All other players are considered in the **backfield** or behind the line of scrimmage. Of those players considered in the backfield only one may move before the snap as long as he is not moving toward the line of scrimmage before the snap occurs. This player is said to be **in motion.**

Passing the Ball: The ball may be thrown forward to another player in order to gain yardage. The player catching the ball must be an **eligible receiver**. An eligible player is one who is aligned as the most outside player on the line of scrimmage or one who is aligned in the backfield. Players with jersey numbers 50 through 79 are not allowed to catch a forward pass. You are only allowed one forward pass per play and the passer must be behind the line of scrimmage.

Running the Ball: The quarterback can hand off or toss the ball to the **running backs**. Everyone else will block a defender so the **"back"** can run as far as possible toward the goal line. At times, the quarterback will run with the ball while trying to attempt a pass. This is known as a **scramble**. In this way, he can avoid being **sacked** or tackled behind the line of scrimmage.

Punting the Ball: When the offense does not feel its chances of gaining the 10 yards required for another first down are good, they may choose to punt the ball to the other team. At this time, you see a whole new group of players running onto the field. These are the special teams known as punt and punt return. The player who will kick the ball is called the **punter**. He will stand 12 to 14 yards directly behind a lineman who will snap or pass the ball between his legs directly to him. The punter will catch the ball, drop it directly onto his foot, and kick it as far as possible. The other team will take possession where their **punt catcher** is tackled, or if not caught, where the ball rolls out of bounds or to a stop on the field.

Defense — Stop the Offense from Scoring!

The defense reacts to the offense. They stop the other team — who now has possession of the ball — from scoring. They typically do this by **tackling** the player with the ball, pulling him down or knocking him down. There are rules on how they can do this. For example, a defensive player can't punch, trip, kick, or pull an opponent down by his facemask; this is against the rules and would lead to a penalty.

So despite an initial impression that football is just organized violence or a free-for-all fight on the field, it is actually very controlled and involves a great deal of strength, skill, and strategy to stop the other team with the ball from moving down the field.

The defense is skilled in tackling and **pass coverage** — skills that are practiced over and over in pre-season and daily throughout the season.

Defensive Philosophy: Stop the offense from successfully running the ball. Change where your defenders line up to confuse the offense.

Make the offense run the ball outside the hash marks and throw passes toward the sideline.

Everyone attack the player with the football — eliminate big gains of yards.

As the offense approaches the goal line, make them kick field goals. No touchdowns.

> **Create turnovers. Get the ball so your offense can score points or score points yourself.**

Cause the offense to **fumble the ball**. Hard tackling and grabbing at the ball will force the offense to drop the ball on the ground and gives the defense a chance to take possession of the ball.

Intercept the ball. Catch passes thrown by the other team.

Sack the passer!!!

Blitz the quarterback when he is attempting to pass. Do this by sending more defenders after the quarterback than the offense has blockers when he is trying to pass. Defense can either tackle the quarterback before he has a chance to throw the ball, resulting in a big loss of yards and maybe a fumble or…

Force him to make a bad throw which will lead to an **interception**.

Okay, so now that you understand what the offensive and defensive teams are doing, what should you focus on while watching the game? With so much action, here are just a few suggestions for what to look at during the game:

Keep your eye on the ball.

- **Watch what happens** when the team is faced with fourth down. Chances are good they will punt the ball, but in some cases, when they are close to making 10 yards, they will "go for it," or if they are close enough to the goal, they will try to kick a field goal.
- **Try to anticipate** what the next play will be — what the quarterback will do with the ball on the next play (throw it deep down field or short, or hand it to the running back).
- **Watch for the defense** to gamble and send extra pass rushers after the quarterback while he is passing in order to sack the quarterback.
- **Pick a player** on the field and watch what he does for three straight plays.
- **Watch one of the coaches** on the sideline — his mannerisms, expressions (they're hilarious).

- **Find the other team's coach** when something goes bad for them.
- **Watch the umpire,** since he is the official standing in the middle of the action between the linebackers on defense. You'll see him move to get out of the way and sometimes he gets knocked down.

Penalties — Hey! You can't do that!

When someone does something that is against the rules (known as a **foul**), the official will announce a **penalty** against the team. Penalties typically are grouped as 5-yard, 10-yard, or 15-yard penalties and allow you to replay the down (first, second, third, or fourth) you just used. The big four:

Illegal Procedure or Movement (Offense) — Can't move suddenly forward until the ball moves. (Minus 5 yards from the line of scrimmage, replay the down.)

Offside's (Defense) — Can't cross the line of scrimmage until the ball moves. (Plus 5 yards from the line of scrimmage, replay the down.)

Holding (Offense) — Can't grab and hold defenders when blocking. (Minus 10 yards from the spot of the foul, replay the down.)

Pass Interference (Defense) — Can't touch pass catchers while the pass is in the air until the ball is touched. (Plus 15 yards or spot of the foul if less than 15 yards, automatic first down.)

NOTE: *There are many other fouls and penalties in the game of football, but if you know the big four, your knowledge will be solid. If you don't understand what foul has been called or what the penalty is for, this is a great time to ask the person you are with so he or she can share his or her knowledge of the game with you!*

Accepting or Declining Penalties — Each foul has a penalty associated with it, which can mean a loss of yardage. However, the offense will be able to replay the previous down.

• • • • • • • • • • • • • • • • • •

The other team has the choice of accepting the penalty or declining the enforcement of the penalty.

An example of a reason to decline a penalty would be:

A foul was called on third down against the offense and without the penalty the offense will be faced with fourth down and **long yardage** (they would have a long way to go to make the first down). Knowing that the offense will elect to punt the ball on fourth down, it is better for the defense to decline the penalty that was called against the offense. This will force the offense to punt instead of giving them another chance to replay the third down and achieve a first down and 10 yards.

Scoring: Run, Pass or Kick

This is easy to understand

6 points: Touchdown
1 point: PAT - Kick Extra Point
2 points: PAT - Go for Two
3 points: Field goal
2 points: Safety

Touchdown (6 points): While holding the ball, cross the facing goal line.

Points After Touchdown (PAT): The ball is placed at the 3-yard line. This is referred to as a **try** — meaning the team that has just scored a touchdown is going to try for additional points with one of two tactics:

Kick the Extra Point (1 point) — The offense's special team for kicking will line up close together along the line of scrimmage. The **kick holder** will kneel down 7 yards from the ball. The kicker is behind the holder.

The ball is snapped directly to the holder, who places the ball on the ground and the kicker kicks the ball up into the air and between the upright poles of the goal post.

Go for Two (2 points) — The ball may be placed anywhere the offense chooses between the hash marks. They then execute a play called in the huddle. If the ball crosses the goal line in possession of the offense, they are awarded two points.

However… The defense is awarded 2 points if they block the extra point kick and return it all the way to the opposite goal line or, on the try for two they return a fumble or interception to the opposite goal line.

3 POINTS

Field Goal (3 points): On fourth down, when the offense does not feel good about its chances of gaining the 10 yards required for another first down, they may choose to attempt a field goal if they are close enough to the goal post. They will line up with the same **formation** used to kick the extra point and the kicker once again must kick the ball through the goal post's **uprights**. If the kick is **no good**, the other team will take possession from the previous line of scrimmage if attempted outside the 20-yard line and at the 20-yard line if the kick was attempted inside the 20. If the kick is blocked and returned to the opposite goal line by the defense, the team is awarded a touchdown and has the chance to score a PAT (Points After Touchdown).

Safety (2 points): While holding the ball, you are tackled behind the goal line at your back. The official will signal a safety by placing his arms above his head (like the score signal) except his palms will be pressed together.

2 POINTS

If the game is tied at the end of the fourth period, **overtime** begins with a new coin toss. It is to a team's advantage to choose to play defense first so they know what is required of the offense once they get the ball.

For example, if the other team goes first and they score a field goal, the team going next knows they need to score a touchdown to win or a field goal to tie the score.

Each team is given the ball at the 25-yard line and one opportunity to score. If both teams score the same amount of points, a second overtime is played. They switch ends of the field and the other team gets to play first. This continues until one team outscores the other. After three overtimes, if a team scores a touchdown, they lose the option of kicking an extra point and must go for two, which is more difficult and more likely to lead to a winner.

SECTION V:

AFTER THE GAME

The players attend a short team meeting back in the locker room so that the head coach can give post-game observations of how he felt about the game. Then the media is invited to ask questions of the head coach and some selected players at an organized **press conference**. The game statisticians present the media with the official statistics for the game and a play-by-play description. The media use these statistics to report on the game later.

Despite years of training, at the end of the day - or in this case, at the end of this football game - it all comes down to who scored the most points. Wins versus losses. Yes, statistics are kept on individual and team leaders, and in some cases, teams will make a post-season game or even a bowl game, and some players will rise to become the nation's leading scorer, rusher, or passer, but few players will ever be recognized on the national level. Of the hundreds of college football teams, only one will become the national champion. And of the thousands of college football players, only a handful are picked to be on the **All-American Team**, which identifies the best football players in each position. And only one of these players will be chosen as the top college football player in the country, receiving the **Heisman Trophy**. Most players will end their football careers with graduation from college, since so few (2.4%) are chosen to go on to play professional football.

Bowl Games

Bowl games typically refer to post-season games. While there are dozens of bowl games, probably the most recognized are those sponsored by the **Bowl Championship Series (BCS)**:

- **Fiesta Bowl**
- **Orange Bowl**
- **Rose Bowl**
- **Sugar Bowl**

While bowl games offer student-athletes the chance to compete in the postseason, they also generate large amounts of excitement and revenues to the individual schools participating in these bowl games. The season comes to an end when the two top-rated teams in the BCS meet in a final bowl game to determine the national champion. **The Coaches' Trophy** is awarded by the **American Football Coaches Association** to the winner.

SECTION VI:

LISTENING TO THE GAME

When a football game is aired on television or radio, it usually involves two people describing the action. One is the **play-by-play commentator**, who tells you exactly what is happening on the field, and the other is the **color commentator,** who adds interesting statistics or a critique of the play. In addition to the terms found in **bold** throughout this book (e.g., blitz, down marker, holding, in motion), there are other terms you may hear used by these commentators when you listen to a college football game, including:

Breakaway — the player carrying the ball gets past the other team and runs toward the goal line for a score.

Big play — a play that gets 15 or more yards.

Bootleg — the quarterback fakes a hand off to a running back and runs with ball in the opposite direction, looking to pass it to a receiver.

Broken play — miscommunication and confusion about what play was called, usually resulting in lost yardage.

Clipping — blocking a defender from behind, resulting in a 15-yard penalty.

Corner — it refers to a player, but also is a pass route in which a receiver runs to a specific area to catch the ball, usually into the middle of the field, then turns and runs back toward the sideline in order to catch a pass.

Cutting against the grain/Radical cutback/Reversing the field — when a runner with the ball stops suddenly and changes direction back toward the chasing defenders in order to surprise them before they can change direction and make the tackle.

Deep downfield — throwing or kicking the ball far down the field.

Draw — the quarterback fakes the pass and hands it to a running back.

Fair catch — the punt team kicks the ball to the punt return team and the catcher waves his hand above his head before catching the ball to signal that he will not run with the ball after he catches it.

False start — a slang term for an illegal procedure foul by the offense.

First-and-10 - short for first down and 10 yards to go.

Going wide — the player runs with the ball toward the sideline.

Gridiron — refers to North American football since the playing field, with its parallel lines, resembles a metal grate for grilling or gridiron.

Hail Mary pass — usually the last play of the game, it is a desperate attempt to score a touchdown by throwing the ball into the end zone from far away.

Hang time — how long the ball is in the air after it has been kicked.

Hole — an opening created between defenders that allows an offensive player with the ball to get past would-be tacklers.

I formation —how running backs line up in the backfield directly behind the quarterback, one behind another.

Incomplete pass — a pass that is not caught or it is batted down by a defender.

Lateral — a backward pass.

Live ball/Loose ball — no one is holding the football and it can be recovered by the offense or defense.

Loss of down — a penalty that does not allow you to replay the down and includes loss of yards, associated with an illegal forward pass.

Man-to-man coverage — a defensive back covers a receiver one-on-one.

Nose tackle — the defensive tackle lines up directly opposite the center on the offense who snaps the ball.

Off tackle — a running play behind the offensive tackle.

Onside kick — a form of kickoff used to surprise the other team and give the offense a chance to recover the ball because it is only kicked 10 yards along the ground.

Outside zone — a running play toward the sideline where blockers block any defender in their area.

Over the middle — a pass thrown in the middle of the field.

Overthrow — a pass thrown too far for the receiver to catch.

Personal foul — a violation for misconduct.

Pocket — area formed by blocking linemen where the quarterback stands to throw a pass directly behind the center.

Run out the clock — running plays designed to keep the game clock running when a team has the lead.

Return yardage — the yards gained by a player after catching a kick.

Rushing — yards gained running with the football.

Screen pass — short pass behind the line of scrimmage where the quarterback draws the defensive lineman toward him before releasing the ball, allowing the offensive line to get in front of the pass catcher and block defenders down field.

Shotgun — the quarterback lines up 5 yards behind the center to receive the snap, usually to pass the ball.

Signals — hand gestures from the coaches to tell the players what play or defense to run.

Sweep play — a run toward the sideline with offensive linemen in front of the ball carrier to block for him.

Third and long — third down and the offense needs to gain 8 or more yards.

Total yardage — yards gained through the course of the game.

Turnovers — the offense loses possession of the ball and the other team gets it through a fumble or interception.

Zone coverage — opposite of man-to-man in which each player on defense covers a particular area (zone) of the field when the offense is trying to pass the ball.

We invite you to send us questions you still have about the game or aspects you would find helpful so we can consider them for possible inclusion in our next edition. tackling-football.com

About The Authors

Sandra L. Caron is a Professor of Family Relations and Human Sexuality at the University of Maine. She has been both professionally and personally involved in college athletics. She is a graduate of the University of Maine and Syracuse University. She has served as a member of the University of Maine Athletic Advisory Board for more than a decade, coordinator of the Faculty Liaison Program for the Athletic Department, and director of Athletes for Sexual Responsibility, a nationally recognized peer education program that trains student-athletes to educate others on sexuality issues. Personally, she has been an avid, but average, college football fan for more than three decades.

J. Michael Hodgson has more than 30 years of experience with college football, including his role as a player and a football coach for several colleges. He played football for the University of Maine where he was a three-year starter at tight end and also handled place kicking duties. He began his coaching career there, working with tight ends, the offensive line, and running backs before moving to Princeton University as wide receivers coach and the passing game coordinator. He went on to become head coach for Maine Maritime Academy. He was the offensive coordinator and quarterbacks/wide receivers coach at Central Connecticut State University, and then served as quarterbacks and receivers coach at Edinboro University in Pennsylvania. Most recently, he was offensive coordinator and running backs/tight ends coach for Dartmouth College.

Made in the USA
Lexington, KY
11 September 2011